People of Scotland 2

Dorothy Morrison

Oliver & Boyd

Introduction

The stories in this book are about people who lived long ago. Their lives are part of the history of Scotland. Perhaps some of them lived near where you stay. Every place has a history made by the people who lived and worked there. Your mother and father have helped to make yesterday's history. What you do will become part of history too. You are part of the story of the people of Scotland.

Teachers' Note

These stories introduce some of the main features of the history of Scotland in the last 200 years. Scots men and women have made an important contribution to modern society through their inventions, exploration and service abroad and the part they have played in medicine, politics, sport and the arts. These, together with major developments of the first Industrial Revolution in steam power, transport, the mining and textile industries are presented in a very simple way through stories. All the stories are based on historical evidence. They describe incidents which actually happened. Stories from various parts of the country have been included to show the wide variety of incident and location which is part of the people of Scotland.

Contents

1. A Sunday Walk

Glasgow Green was busy, for it was a fine Sunday afternoon. Many people were taking a walk or stopping to talk to friends.

James Watt strolled through the gate at the foot of Charlotte Street. As he passed the old washing house he stopped suddenly. The people who were walking behind him stopped too.

"What's wrong? What's he looking at?" a girl asked her brother.

"It must be something in here," he said as he peered into the washing house. "But I can't see anything."

James Watt walked slowly on bumping into two well-dressed ladies coming the other way. He did not notice.

"That young man is speaking to himself!" one said loudly.

"He should watch where he's going!" said the other crossly.

James did not hear. He was too busy thinking.

On he walked past the herd's house, nearly knocking down a rather stout old gentleman. By this time several people were watching him. Every time he stopped suddenly, people close behind had to step aside. Children began to walk alongside staring up at him.

"I do believe I have solved the problem at last," James thought. "As soon as I get to work tomorrow I'll start on a steam engine that will really work well. Why, it could change everything!"

He still did not notice that a crowd of people had gathered. Thinking deeply he stood in the middle of the path.

Then, smiling happily, James Watt turned back towards home.

"I wonder what all these folk are staring at?" he thought as he made his way towards the gate." "I don't see anything strange. Anyway, it can't be me they're looking at. I've done nothing odd. I've just been thinking."

A Sunday Walk

To make machines work power is needed.

When James Watt was a boy in Greenock he could see many different kinds of machines.

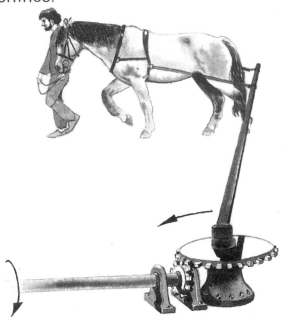

Some machines were worked by hand.

Sometimes animals helped.

Mills often used water power.

The wind helped to work machines too.

Steam Power

James learned how to make very fine tools. One day he was asked to repair a model engine worked by steam. The machine did not work well. Watt thought about this for many months. He worked out how to make a much better steam engine.

Luckily he found rich men who could help to pay for making the new engine. His engine could be used to work all kinds of machines. It changed the way people worked. Instead of working at home, many people went to work in factories full of machines worked by steam. Steam engines were used in the mines and even on farms. Other men made steam trains and steam ships. People could travel faster than ever before.

James Watt became famous as an inventor all over the world. He was one of Scotland's greatest engineers.

2. A Ruined Home

"Stop a minute, Gilbert!" shouted Robert Burns to his brother as they reached the end of the ridge.

Gilbert halted the horses and came round to the plough.

"Look at this," said Robert as he picked up some withered grasses.

It was a bleak, cold day. The rain and sleet had stopped but now a biting wind was blowing over the valley. Gilbert wanted to finish his work and get home. "It's only a nest some mouse has made, Rab," he said angrily. "It's not worth stopping for."

Robert had been watching the plough carefully to see that no rocks or stones got in the way. Just near the end of the furrow he had seen a small, brown shape dart out in front of him. The timid, little mouse was in a panic.

"What a shame!" thought Robert as he gently turned over the grasses which had been woven together with such care. "This poor wee mouse spent so long making itself a cosy shelter. It thought it was safe from rain and wind and frost. Then my plough came through."

"You know, Gilbert," he said, "a mouse is part of life as much as we are. This wee beastie didn't know that suddenly its well-planned house would be ruined. We never know when things might go wrong for us too."

"Forget about it Rab," said Gilbert. "Let's get finished and go home."

Robert Burns didn't forget. That night as he sat by the fire he wrote a poem. It was called 'To a Mouse'.

A Ruined Home

Robert Burns lived in Ayrshire. Although he was a farmer, he loved to write poetry in the Scots language.

This is the first verse of Robert's poem about the mouse.

Wee, sleekit, cow'rin', tim'rous beastie,
Oh, what a panic's in thy breastie!
Thou need na start awa sae hasty,
       Wi' bickering brattle!
I wad be laith to rin an' chase thee,
       Wi' murd'ring pattle!

When a book of his poems was printed, Robert Burns became well-known in Scotland. All the important people in Edinburgh made a fuss of him. He wrote many more poems but he did not make much money.

Young Walter Scott sees Robert Burns meet other famous writers in Edinburgh

Burns' Night

Today Burns is famous all over the world. Every year on 25th January, people meet to remember his birthday. After a supper of haggis, turnips and mashed potatoes, they read the poems and sing the songs which Burns wrote.

Everyone drinks a toast to the memory of the famous Scots poet.

3. The Tumble-down Church

"Every time it rains, all the people in the church get wet through," said the vicar. "The roof badly needs repair."

The young Scots surveyor picked his way slowly round the grave-stones. They came right up to the walls of the church. Every now and then he stopped to look up at the tower. He peered closely at the cracks which ran up the wall.

"The meeting in the tower room would like to hear your report," said the vicar.

Thomas Telford nodded. Looking in the door of the tower he said, "I will stay and talk only if the meeting is held out here in the churchyard."

"This is not a joking matter, young man," snapped a church member. "In England we take church affairs seriously!"

"I'm not joking!" said Telford. "As long as you stay in the church you are in danger. It could fall down at any time!"

"Nonsense!" muttered the people in the tower room looking round at the old walls. "These cracks have been there for years. This Scotsman is just trying to make a big job for himself."

They decided only one pillar needed repair and asked a local builder to do the job.

A few days later, very early in the morning, the workmen stood outside the church. One man had gone to get the key. The church clock began to strike. ONE—TWO—THREE—As the clock struck four there was a great crash! The tower swayed for a moment and fell into the centre of the building. The church was a complete ruin!

Luckily no one was hurt, but from then on the people of Shropshire always listened to the advice of Thomas Telford, the young man from Dumfries.

The Tumble-down Church

Thomas Telford was born near Dumfries in Scotland. His father died when Thomas was very young. The family was poor. His mother arranged for Thomas to learn the trade of a stone-mason when he was thirteen. Later he went to England to find work and became a very famous builder. He made fine buildings, bridges, docks and harbours in England and Scotland.

Telford's Roads

When Telford was young, travelling was difficult. Journeys took a long time. The roads were rough and uneven. In wet weather they were muddy. In dry weather there was dust everywhere. Telford tried to build good roads. First he told his workers to dig a solid base for the road. Then they put big stones at the bottom. There were smaller stones on top. The water could drain away after the rain.

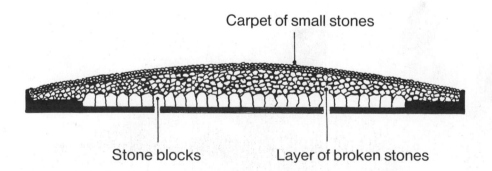

Carpet of small stones

Stone blocks   Layer of broken stones

There were few roads in the Highlands of Scotland. Now there are bridges and roads which he built all over Scotland.

The Caledonian Canal

It was hard for sailors to travel round the north of Scotland. Ships were wrecked if there was a bad storm. To help them Telford made a canal. It cut right across Scotland. The Caledonian Canal joined the North Sea to the Atlantic.

Telford's Achievements

Telford worked all his life building roads and bridges. By the time he was an old man travel was much better. He had built 1200 bridges and over 1700 kilometres of good roads.

Locks on the Caledonian Canal at Fort Augustus

The Menai Suspension Bridge was made of iron. It joins two parts of Wales together.

4. The Boy Convict

There was a jingle of keys. The cell door opened.
Prisoners' names were called out, and the convicts
were marched off, all chained together. People
lined the streets to watch them pass.

Andrew felt very afraid. It was just three weeks
since his trial. He had set fire to some straw for a
prank. The magistrate had been very stern.

"We must make an example of young criminals
like you. You will be transported to Australia for
seven years. You are only sixteen. Perhaps hard
work in a new land will help you to grow into a
better man."

Now Andrew was a convict.

The prisoners were loaded into boats at the
jetty and rowed out to the dark old sailing ship
waiting in the bay. Andrew had never been in a
ship before—his home was in the Borders. As he
climbed the ladder to go on board he turned to
look back.

"Move along there!" shouted a guard. "You've
had your last look at the old country!"

Andrew tried hard not to cry, as he stumbled
forward. There were over 400 prisoners. As their
names were checked off, they were taken below
deck.

Andrew was crowded into a large iron cage. It was very hot and stuffy. There was hardly room to sit down. This was to be his home for the next seven months.

For two more days the ship lay at anchor. Then one day there was great noise and shouting. With a loud creak the old ship began to move. Some prisoners cried out. Others wept quietly. Some banged angrily on the bars of the cage. Andrew stood still and silent. He knew he had left home for ever.

Andrew, the convict, was bound for Australia.

The Boy Convict

Many of the convicts sent to
Australia were poor men. It was
hard to find work. Men often stole
food for their families. Some
caught fish or birds or rabbits
which belonged to the owner of
the land.

Some men joined together to try
to change the way the country
was run. When any of these
people were caught they were
harshly treated.

Convicts boarding the ship which
will take them to Australia

Prisoners (in cages) on board ship

The *Pitt* on which Andrew sailed took 212 days to reach Australia. He often felt sick. Over fifty people died on the journey. Some had smallpox or bad fevers. Disease spread quickly when people were crowded together.

Andrew worked very hard in Australia. He did so well that he was set free after four years. He got a good job and was given land.

Although he became rich, Andrew was never able to return to Scotland.

The life in Australia was hard. Andrew died when he was only thirty-five years old.

5. A Good Idea

The guard on the back of the mail coach blew his
horn. With a crack of his whip the coachman
drove swiftly out of the yard. The mail from
Dundee was on its way! James Chalmers noticed
his friend John White among the crowd near the
Post Office.

"Come along to the shop!" he cried taking hold
of John's arm. "I want to show you my latest idea.
I've just sent a letter to London about it."

"What is it this time?" John wondered. "James
is always trying something new. Last year it was
a new kind of fishing tackle. The year before it
was making his own newspaper."

James led his friend through his bookshop into the workroom at the back. His printers were busy setting up type. Going over to his desk, he turned the lock and opened a drawer. Smiling to himself he took out a sheet of paper printed on one side.

"What do you think of that, John?" he asked. "It's a trial run. If the government take up my idea it will make it easy to send a letter."

"Very nice, I'm sure," replied John looking at the paper in a puzzled way. "But what exactly is it?"

"Feel the back!" James ordered.

"It's sticky," said his friend.

"Correct!" said Chalmers eagerly. "It's a new sticky postage stamp!"

A Good Idea

James Chalmers of Dundee invented the first postage stamp which could be stuck on a letter. He printed it on his own printing press.

Chalmer's printing press

These pictures show how letters were sent long ago.

1.

The sheet of paper was folded. Then it was turned round and folded twice more.

2.
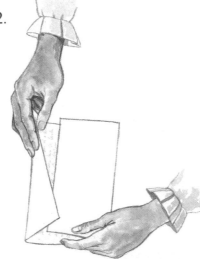

One end was tucked inside the other.

3.

The address was written with a quill pen.

4. A blotter was used to dry the ink.

5. Melted sealing wax was dropped on the join of the letter. A seal was pressed on the hot wax.

It cost a lot to send a letter then. It might be as much as a day's wages for a working man. It was the person who received a letter who had to pay for it. Letters cost more the further they went. Often poor people could not afford to pay for a letter.

In England a man called Rowland Hill said that more people would use the post if it was cheaper. Then the Post Office would make more money. James Chalmers wrote to Hill to tell him of his idea for a sticky postage stamp.

Penny Post

In 1840 the first Penny Post began. Everyone was pleased. Now people could pay to send their letters cheaply. Within ten years five times as many letters were being posted. The idea was a great success.

James Chalmers' idea of a stamp that was sticky on the back was used, but Rowland Hill got all the credit.

It was over 130 years later before the Post Office agreed that the man who first thought of a sticky postage stamp was James Chalmers of Dundee.

The Penny Black, an early postage stamp

6. A Hard Life

Eleven-year-old Rebecca Simpson was crying as she staggered up the steep slope. The rope tied to the coal cart dragged tightly on her waist. She knew she must not stop. Her younger sister, Nell, was pushing from behind. She might be crushed if the heavy cart ran backwards.

"You're nae pushin' hard enough!" she shouted. "We'll no' get the cart up the brae!"

All at once the cart moved forward. Their brother George had come to help.

"Get a move on," he grumbled. "Faither's near ready to load up again."

24

Rebecca sighed and struggled on. She peered into the dark. The candle on the cart did not give much light. The rough floor was wet and slippery.

When the girls reached the bottom of the pit shaft, their mother was waiting. A large flat basket lay on the ground. They loaded the largest pieces of coal into it. Two men strained to lift the heavy weight on to Mrs Simpson's back. Bent almost double, she moved slowly towards the steps to begin the long steep climb to the top.

Rebecca and her sister hurried back with the cart to the coal face where their father hewed the coal. He would be angry if they wasted time.

"How can we make enough to live on if you lassies are so slow?" he would shout.

"Hurry up or I'll take my belt tae ye!"

At last five o'clock came. The two girls had been at work for twelve hours. Now they made their way wearily home.

"Thank goodness it's not a Friday," Rebecca thought. "Then I would have to work all night as well until twelve o'clock on Saturday. It's a hard life down the pit."

A Hard Life

In some parts of Scotland 150 years ago children worked down the mines. They worked with their mothers and fathers. Work began when they were six or seven years old.

The work was very hard. The mines were dark and wet. Sometimes gas would choke the workers.

Children being lowered down to work in the mine

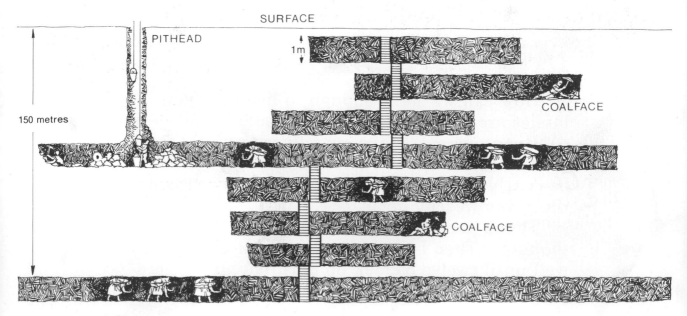

SURFACE

PITHEAD

1m

150 metres

COALFACE

COALFACE

Miners had to crawl along narrow passages. There was no room to stand up.

A miner's wife carried heavy baskets of coal on her back. A leather band round her head kept the basket in place.

Often miners were hurt or even killed. Rebecca's brother, Joe, aged twelve, was killed when a piece of the mine roof fell on his head.

People were shocked when they learned about life in the coal pits.

In 1842 a new law stopped women and young children working below ground in the mines.

7. The Devil on Wheels

Two women stood chatting in a shop doorway in New Cumnock. Suddenly they stopped speaking and stared in amazement. What was this coming down the road?

A man on horseback pulled sharply on the reins as his horse bolted in alarm. A young boy raced up the street shouting for his friends to come and look. By the time Mr Macmillan the blacksmith had stopped at the inn, a large crowd had gathered.

"Where did you get that queer machine?" asked one of the boys boldly. "What is it?"

Kirkpatrick Macmillan looked proudly at the two-wheeled cycle on which he had travelled 64 kilometres in only five hours. The heavy wooden frame was covered in dust.

"I made it," he said quietly. "It's a velocipede."

Early the next morning he set off for Glasgow 48 kilometres further on. Once again he caused great excitement.

"It's the devil on wheels!" one man shouted.

As he rode through the Gorbals, a little girl at the front of the crowd was pushed forward. The velocipede bumped into her and she fell to the ground. She began to cry. At once everyone blamed the blacksmith. The little girl was not hurt. As he tried to explain that there was no danger from his machine, he felt a hand on his shoulder.

"You're under arrest!" said a stern voice.

Next day Mr Macmillan was called before a magistrate. "A very interesting case," said the magistrate. "I think I must see how this strange machine works."

He watched carefully as the blacksmith showed how to ride the velocipede. "I'm afraid I must find you guilty," he said. "You did knock the child down. I fine you five shillings." (25p)

Kirkpatrick Macmillan looked sad.

"Don't worry," said the magistrate. "I'll pay the fine myself. Tell me, could you make me one of these exciting machines?"

The Devil on Wheels

Hobby-horses

Many men had made machines with two wheels on which to ride. They looked like the one in this picture. You can see that it has a saddle on a beam that joins two wheels. These machines were called hobby-horses. The rider had to push himself along with his feet.

Kirkpatrick Macmillan lived in the country. He worked as a blacksmith for the Duke of Buccleuch. One day a man brought a hobby-horse to be repaired. The blacksmith was interested. With a machine like this he could travel around more quickly. He looked at it carefully and decided he could make something better.

The First Bicycle

The machine he made had more parts. It had pedals fixed to rods to turn the wheels. But he still had to pull himself along with his feet to start off. He made some spiked shoes to help him get a good grip. The shoes helped him to get round sharp corners too.

Once the machine had started off, he could drive it forward without having to touch the ground with his feet. It was the first bicycle.

The blacksmith did not make much money out of his invention. He let other people copy his idea. Thomas McCall, a joiner from Kilmarnock, made the machine even better. One of his machines, which he sold for £7, is now in the Science Museum in London.

8. The Frightened Patient

John McPherson, the Highlander, was afraid. How he wished he was back in the glen instead of this strange city!

As he limped into the room he was leaning heavily on a stick. Two days before he had fallen badly while at work. His leg was so swollen that his wife had cut a large slit in his trousers. He had only agreed to come to the Royal Infirmary in Edinburgh because he was in great pain.

The surgeon ran his hands gently over John's leg. He looked at it for a long time. At last he said, "I'm afraid I will have to operate. Your leg is broken. It has become badly poisoned too."

John stared at him. He did not understand.

A young doctor stepped forward. "Excuse me, sir," he said to the surgeon, "this man speaks little English. He is from the Highlands. Shall I explain to him?"

Speaking quickly in Gaelic the doctor told John what was going to happen.

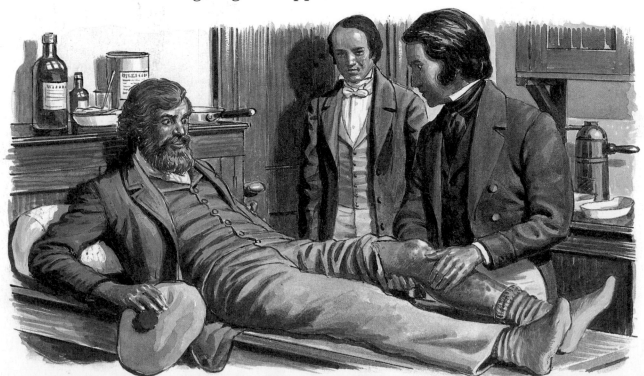

At once the Highlander turned pale. He gripped the edge of the table in panic. He knew people sometimes died because the pain of an operation was so great. To make them keep still they had to be strapped to a table.

"I don't think I could stand it, doctor," he said in his own language. "I could not bear to watch you cut my leg no matter how quick you were. My leg hurts a lot just now. The pain of an operation would be a hundred times worse."

James Simpson the surgeon smiled. "Tell him he need not worry," he said to the young doctor. "After all our tests we know how to help." The other doctors standing beside him nodded and smiled at John.

"You won't feel any pain at all," the young doctor explained. "In fact you will sleep right through the operation. When you wake up you will feel quite well."

"I hope this man knows what he's talking about," thought John, "but at least he's a Highlander like myself."

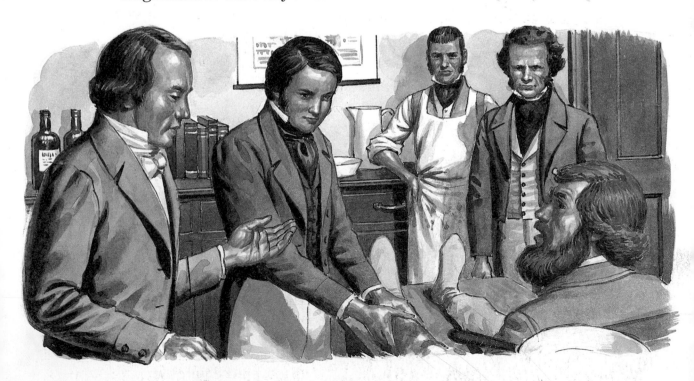

The Frightened Patient

Highlanders forced
to leave their homes

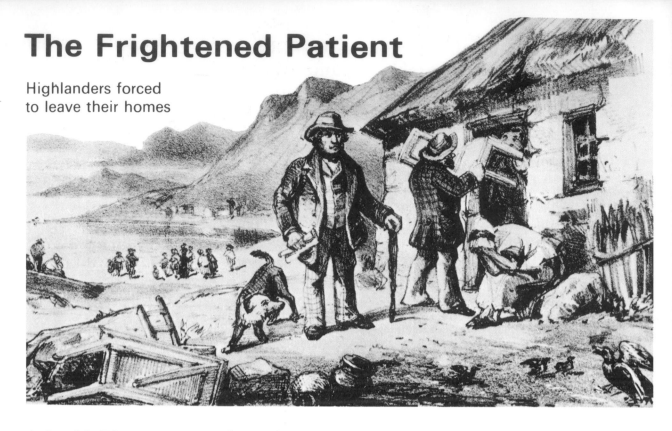

John McPherson came from the Highlands of Scotland. Life was hard there 150 years ago. Some lairds had put sheep on the land. They did not need so many people. Families left the Highlands to look for work. Some went to other lands across the sea. Some, like John, went to work in factories in the towns.

At one time all the people of the Highlands spoke Gaelic. In some places nowadays people can speak both English and Gaelic. Perhaps you can speak Gaelic or know some Gaelic words. A special contest called the Mod is held every year at which Gaelic poetry and songs are heard.

Operations 130 Years Ago

If you had an operation long ago, it hurt a lot. There was no way of putting you to sleep while it was being done.

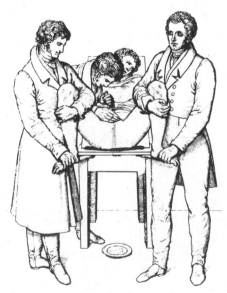

An operation before Simpson discovered chloroform

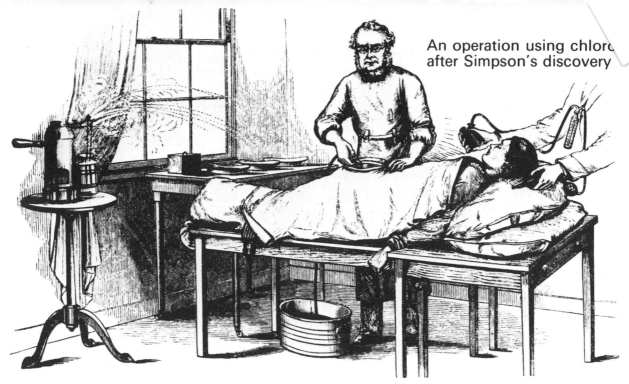

An operation using chlor[oform]
after Simpson's discovery

James Young Simpson, a very clever doctor from Bathgate, found a way to help. He invited friends to his home in Queen Street in Edinburgh. They tried using a drug called chloroform to put each other to sleep.

When it worked well, Simpson used it on patients too. Now he could take more time to operate and know that the patient would not feel pain.

Even Queen Victoria used the drug in 1853 when she had a baby.

Because Simpson had helped so many people who needed to have operations he was honoured. He became Sir James Young Simpson.

Queen Victoria

Sir James Young Simps[on]

9. Sending a Message

"Where are you?" shouted Aleck's father. "Come here at once!"

Hidden behind the big wardrobe, Aleck Bell felt very frightened. He had told his father a lie. There was sure to be trouble.

Mr Brown who was staying at the Bell's home for a few days had been writing letters. Aleck had looked at the paper he had left on the desk. He would write a letter too!

Since he was only five, Aleck could not write. He scribbled all over a page and put it in an envelope. Then he stuck one of Mr Brown's stamps on it. "Please post this for me, Bella," he asked the servant who was dusting the room.

Bella laughed. Aleck's father who was passing looked in. He laughed too at Aleck's letter. Then he said, "Where did you get the stamp?"

"Mother gave it to me," replied Aleck turning red.

Mr Bell looked grave. "Are you sure? Ask your mother to come here," he said.

At once Aleck rushed upstairs to hide. He squeezed in behind a big wardrobe. Everyone in the family looked for him. Through a crack in the wardrobe Aleck watched his mother search among the hanging clothes. He could see his father looking under the bed. His brothers looked behind the curtains. Aleck thought his heart was beating so loudly they would be sure to hear it. All day he stayed in his hiding place. He felt very hungry and tired but he was scared to come out.

When it grew dark, his father became very worried. Had Aleck gone outside? Mr Bell stood in the hall and shouted, "Aleck, come out and I will forgive you!"

Still Aleck did not move. The house was searched again. This time his mother found him. He was so tightly wedged that the wardrobe had to be moved from the wall.

"Why did you do it?" asked his father sternly as the little boy cried in his mother's arms.

"I wanted to send a message!" sobbed Aleck.

Sending a Message

Aleck's name was Alexander Graham Bell. He was born in Edinburgh in 1847. His father taught people how to speak well. He studied how people made sounds to talk to one another and wrote a book about it.

When Aleck grew up, he gave speech lessons also. Because his mother was deaf, he knew how hard it was for deaf people to learn to speak.

He did all he could to help deaf people to understand what others were saying by watching their lips. He taught them how to make sounds and be able to talk.

Aleck worked so hard that he became ill. His mother and father took him to America. When he was well again, he began to teach deaf children there. He married a lady who was deaf.

Making Sounds Travel

He wanted to know how sound travels. For many years he worked with a friend to make sounds travel along a wire from one place to another.

On 10 March 1876 he stood in one room and spoke this message through a speaking tube: "Mr Watson, come here! I want to see you!"

Two doors away, at the end of a long corridor, Mr Watson heard.

Alexander Graham Bell had invented the telephone.

Alexander Graham Bell in 1892 at the opening of
the telephone line from New York to Chicago

10. The Strange Red-haired Woman

Mary Slessor, dressed in her best clothes, was on her way to a church meeting. As she turned into the Seagate, she saw a gang of boys coming towards her. Only the week before they had tried to break up the meeting. They had thrown stones and even horse manure at the people who were singing. The biggest boy had a big lead weight on a cord. He swung it round his head towards Mary. If it hit her she would be badly hurt.

Thinking quickly Mary said, "If I can stand still without moving or blinking while you swing that, will you come to the meeting?"

She took off her hat showing her bright red hair. The gang made a circle round her. The leader swung the cord. The heavy weight came nearer and nearer. It almost touched her nose. Suddenly the boy stopped.

"She's game, boys," he said. "We'll have to go and sing at the meeting!"

Years later Mary was in Calabar in West Africa. She had gone to tell people about her God, Jesus Christ. One day she saw a young girl tied to sticks in the ground. People stood round in a circle. The chief told Mary the girl had done wrong. Boiling oil would be poured over her.

"No!" cried Mary. She rushed into the circle. A masked man stood over the fire. When he saw Mary, he lifted a ladle of boiling oil and swung it round his head. He moved towards Mary.

"It's just like that Sunday in Dundee," thought Mary. She stood still and stared at the man as he came closer. Nearer and nearer came the ladle. Mary could smell the hot oil. The crowd stood silent. What would happen?

All at once the masked man drew back and turned away. Mary walked up to the chief.

"Please," she said. "Let the girl go free. This is too cruel a punishment."

"This woman with the strange red hair is very brave," thought the chief. "I will let her take the girl."

The Strange Red-haired Woman

Mary Slessor had a hard life in the slums in Dundee.
When she was eleven she went to work in the mills.
Her family of seven lived in a one-roomed house. It
had no water, light or toilet inside.

Her father was often drunk. The
family was short of money for
food and clothes. Mary learned to
be tough. But she knew people
would behave better if they were
well fed and were able to work to
earn money.

Mary Slessor in Africa

Calabar is now part of Nigeria. When Mary went there it had great forests and swamps full of insects. Many people died of fever. Mary felt that some of the people in Calabar had a hard life just like those of Dundee. She tried to help. She went to live with the people of the forests for twenty-eight years.

Mary Slessor in an African village

This helped her to know the African way of doing things. She understood African ideas about gods and the world.

Mary learned to build a mud hut to live in. She knew how to guard against snakes and wild animals. Often she was sick or hungry but she stayed in Calabar.

Many Africans felt that Mary was a friend who would help them whenever she could. They called her "mother of all the peoples".

Mary Slessor (*bottom left*) when an old woman

11. The Shipwreck

Young Tom Peters, the second mate, stood beside the captain of the *Strathmore*. Together they peered into the darkness. They were somewhere east of the Cape of Good Hope, sailing to New Zealand. They did not know that the sailing ship was 48 kilometres off course.

Down below, in their cabins, the passengers tried to sleep. All at once there was a loud crunching noise.

"We've hit the rocks!" cried Tom.

Swiftly the crew tried to launch the lifeboats. Huge waves lashed the deck. Many people were swept overboard into the freezing waters. Everywhere there were cries of fear as the panic-stricken passengers realised what was happening. The first lifeboat, full of women and young children, was turned over. The captain and many others were drowned.

Tom Peters took charge. He shouted orders to the crew as they struggled to launch the other lifeboats. It was hard to float them clear of the sinking ship. Huge waves swept over the bridge.

"Up lads! Keep her off the ship!" Tom cried. "Keep baling or we'll sink! Steer clear of the rocks!"

Somehow Tom managed to get 47 men and one woman safe on shore.

The ship had struck the jagged rocks of the Crozet Islands. No people lived there. In the morning light the castaways looked round at the cold bleak shore. Huge birds flew above them. There were penguins everywhere. The people had no food, no warm clothes and nowhere to shelter.

"No one will ever find us here!" cried Mrs Wordsworth, the lady passenger. "What are we going to do?"

The Shipwreck

Tom Peters came from Arbroath. He had been proud to be second mate on the *Strathmore*. It was a brand new ship. This was its first voyage.

The first day on the island he checked on anything that they could use. They found things washed ashore from the ship.

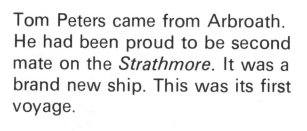

Tom took tins to use as cooking pots. He used the spokes of an umbrella to make needles. They learned to catch birds for food. Clothes were made from penguin skins. Animal fat helped to keep the fire going.

Tom made sure that someone always kept a lookout for a passing ship. Four times they saw ships and tried to signal but the ships sailed on.

They stayed on the island for 194 days. At last, when they had begun to lose hope, an American whaling ship saw their signal. They were saved.

12. A Meeting in the Jungle

It was a hot, dry morning in Ujiji. A white-haired man sat outside a thatched hut. He looked tired and ill.

"Has it all been worth-while?" he wondered to himself.

"It's over thirty years since I first left Britain to come to Africa. I have travelled thousands of miles making maps of my journeys. I have seen places no white man has ever seen before. I love Africa and its people, but I do not think I have really helped them at all.

"Not many listen when I preach about my God. There are still men and women sold as slaves. Traders still cheat and kill the people.

"Now my supplies have been stolen. All my medicines have gone. I have no beads or cloth to use to buy things. I am too weak to travel further.

"I wanted to tell people in Britain what a wonderful country this is. I thought they would

help Africa. It is so long since I could send a message that they will have forgotten all about me."

As the old man sat thinking, his African friend, Susi, came running up.

"I have news," he shouted. "There is a white man asking about you. He has many men with him who carry supplies."

Two days later Henry Morton Stanley, a young newspaper reporter, came to Ujiji. He had been sent all the way from America. His journey had taken him eight months. He had travelled through swamps and forests and met fierce wild animals.

A great crowd gathered round. Susi led the way. The man Stanley had come so far to see stood outside his hut smiling shyly.

Stanley was so happy that he did not know what to say. He took off his hat, held out his hand and said, "Doctor Livingstone, I presume?"

A Meeting in the Jungle

David Livingstone was born
in a room at the top
of this building

David Livingstone was born in
Blantyre near Glasgow in 1813.
His family was poor He lived
with his father, mother, two
brothers and two sisters in a
house with one room.

When David was ten he left
school. He went to work in a
cotton mill twelve hours a day.

A painting of young David Livingstone
at work in the cotton mill

In his spare time he studied hard because he wanted to be able to help other people. By the time he was twenty-three David was able to train as a doctor.

In 1840 Dr Livingstone sailed to Africa. He hoped to teach people about Jesus Christ. Travelling in Africa was very hard. There were no roads. Livingstone had to journey through swamps and jungle.

The rivers were full of crocodiles. Once he was attacked by a lion. Messages and supplies from Britain took a long time to reach him.

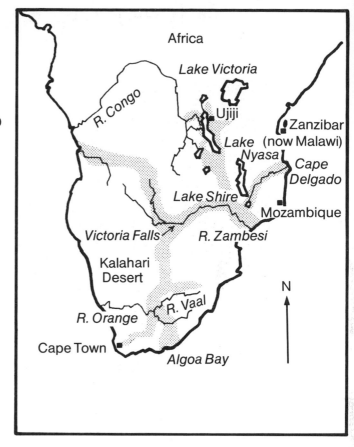

Dr Livingstone's journeys in Africa

Dr Livingstone made friends with African people. In some places men and women were sold as slaves. David wanted to stop this. He tried to find good ways to travel. He made maps to show rivers, forests and lakes.

When he went back to visit Britain, everyone wanted to hear about Africa. But the other men who then came to buy and sell in Africa did not treat the people well. These traders wanted to become rich. They did not help the Africans as David had hoped.

Soon after Stanley's visit David Livingstone died in Africa. His African friends travelled for six months to bring his body to the coast. A ship brought the body to Britain.

Livingstone was so famous as an explorer that he was buried in Westminster Abbey.

13. The New MP

A cheer went up. Everyone strained to see. Keir Hardie was coming!

Through the eager crowd walked a small, bearded man. This was James Keir Hardie's great day. Only a few days before he had won the election against Major Banes by over 1000 votes. Now he was off to Parliament for the first time.

The crowd started to gather early in the morning. Men from the London docks had taken a day off work. They would get no pay but they wanted to see their new Member of Parliament set out. The local gas workers were there ready to cheer. Many Irishmen who lived in London were there as well.

A cart pulled by two horses stood ready. It was decorated with flags and red cloth. When the new MP had climbed on board, it set off slowly. A man on the back played a rousing tune on a trumpet. Everyone cheered and shouted.

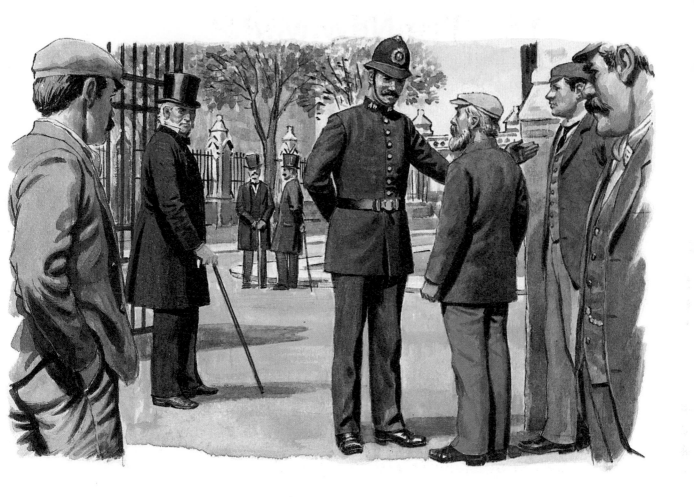

When they arrived at the gates to the Houses of
Parliament, the policeman on duty would not let
the cart go any further. Keir Hardie climbed
down. Other people stopped to stare. Could this be
the new MP?

With his yellow tweed trousers Keir Hardie
wore a serge jacket and a waistcoat. On his head he
wore an ordinary workman's cap. Members of
Parliament always dressed in neat dark suits and
wore hats. A gentleman would not dream of going
anywhere important wearing a cap!

Old Mr Gladstone, the famous leader of the
Liberal party, had been in Parliament a long time.
He looked amazed as he met Keir Hardie going in.

"This is a new kind of MP," he thought.
"Things are really changing in Parliament!"

The New M.P.

People's votes help to decide how the country is run.

The laws which everyone has to obey are made in Parliament. Each area has a Member of Parliament. He is called an MP for short. Everyone over 18 can vote to choose who it will be. This is called an election.

Although he was an MP in London, James Keir Hardie was a Scot. He was born in Holytown in Lanarkshire in 1856. His family was poor and James started work in the mines when he was ten years old. For thirteen years he worked as a miner.

He went to school at night to learn as much as he could. This helped him to speak well in front of other people.

He often spoke at church meetings. Many people had to work very hard for low wages. Sometimes they took too much to drink. It helped them to forget how unpleasant life was. Keir Hardie told them to drink less, read more and think more.

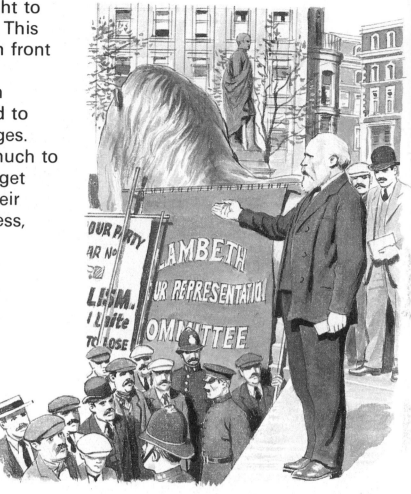

When Keir Hardie became an MP he got no pay. It was hard for a working man to be in Parliament. Other workers had to help gather money to pay for someone to speak up for them.

Keir Hardie thought men should not have to work more than eight hours every day. He said that richer people should pay tax. The money they paid would help to give old people a pension to live on.

Many people had no job. Keir Hardie spoke in Parliament of their problems and hardships so that he was called "The member for the unemployed".

14. Women on the March

The procession was coming. Little Mary could hear music. People were singing. Mary was so small she could not see over the heads of the crowd. Her big sister Jessie picked her up.

A long line of women was coming along the road. Some carried banners as they marched. Others had posies of flowers. A small plump lady riding a large white horse proudly led the way. She had a cap like a soldier's on her head. The big white sash on her tunic said, "VOTES FOR WOMEN!"

"Why are there no men in the march?" Mary asked her sister.

The old man standing next to them looked angry. "You are too young to understand," he grumbled. "It's just women's nonsense. These Suffragettes will be wanting to do men's jobs next!"

"Is that wrong?" Mary asked.

"Of course it is," he replied. "Women should stick to the kitchen. They don't know how to run the country. Their job is to look after a home and family. Women will never be allowed to vote."

"Look Mary," Jessie said eagerly. "There's the General! That's Flora Drummond! She's one of the Suffragette leaders."

As she passed the children Flora Drummond smiled and waved.

Jessie began to cheer. "Votes for women!" she shouted.

Women on the March

Flora Drummond was born in 1879 in Arran in Scotland. When she was a young girl, it was hard for women to get a good job. Many women worked as servants. Those in shops and factories were not paid as much as men. They were not allowed to vote for an MP.

Flora passed examinations to be a postmistress. Then she was told she was too small for the job. This made her very angry.

When Flora Drummond got married, she went to live in Manchester. Most men did not think women should vote. Her husband was different. He told her to join other women called Suffragettes who wanted votes for women. Their leader was Mrs Pankhurst. The Suffragettes made speeches but few listened. Keir Hardie was one of the few MPs who helped them. They decided to shock people. They began to break windows and to burn letters in pillar boxes.

This banner shows that some men wanted women to have the vote

Left Suffragettes marching in Princes Street, Edinburgh

Some even burned down empty houses. Soon everyone knew about the Suffragettes. Some were put in prison but they did not give in.

Flora Drummond used the water pipes to tap out messages to other prisoners.

In 1914 Britain had to fight in a Great War. Women did all they could to help. Many took over men's jobs so that they could fight. They helped men on the Clyde to build ships. They helped miners at the pit heads. Some became drivers, postwomen and policewomen. Flora Drummond worked hard to help win the war.

Women did so well that when the war was over they were allowed to vote. Some women became MPs.

In 1979 a woman became Prime Minister in charge of the government for the first time.

A suffragette in prison

Flora Drummond in the uniform she invented for herself

Women doing 'men's work' during the Great War

15. A great Day for the Flying Scot

It was a very special day in the University of Edinburgh. Rows of students wearing black gowns looked towards the high platform. This was the day they had waited for. After years of hard work they would be leaving the university with a degree. Their parents and friends had come to see the ceremony. They clapped as the students walked up to the platform one by one when their names were called.

In the third row sat a young man called Eric Liddell. As he walked forward to the Principal of the university there was a great cheer. Everyone stood up to clap loudly. Eric smiled shyly.

The Principal held up his hand to stop the loud cheers. "Mr Liddell," he said smiling, "you have shown that no one can pass you ... except the examiner."

There were more cheers. Everyone understood what he meant. They thought it a good joke.

Eric had studied hard. The examiner at university had given him a pass mark, but people were cheering for another reason. Eric Liddell had become famous as a sportsman. Only six days before he had won a Gold medal at the Olympic Games in Paris. In 47.6 seconds he had run the 400 metre race and finished 5 metres ahead of all the rest. It was a great victory. In the newspapers he was called "The Flying Scot". People in Scotland were thrilled.

The university had arranged a surprise for Eric. Long ago in Ancient Greece the winner at the Olympic Games was crowned with a circle made of olive leaves. A special poem was written in his

honour. Now the Principal placed a ring of olive leaves on Eric's head and gave him a poem in Greek.

A huge crowd of students were waiting for Eric when he left the hall. They put him in a chair and carried him on their shoulders right up the Royal Mile to St Giles Cathedral. All along the street people cheered and waved. "What a fine young man," they said. "What will he do now? He's sure to get a good job. Everyone in Scotland is proud of him!"

That night Eric gave everyone a surprise. At a special dinner he stood up to thank his friends. He would not be staying in Scotland.

"I'm going to be a missionary," he said. "Soon I will be leaving for China."

A Great Day for the Flying Scot

Eric Liddell's mother and father were missionaries in China. Eric was sent home to Britain to go to school and university.

In 1924 he was chosen to run in the 100 m race at the Olympic Games. When he found out he would have to run on a Sunday he would not take part in the race. He felt it was wrong. At that time many people believed that working or playing games should only happen on weekdays. Others were angry with Eric. They had hoped a Scotsman might win.

Eric agreed to run in the 400 m race instead on another day. He won a gold medal for Britain. In 1980 another Scot, Allan Wells, won an Olympic gold medal for the 100 m race. "I ran this one for Eric Liddell," he said.

Alan Wells wins his Olympic gold medal in 1980

In 1925 Eric went to work as a missionary in China. He did not often have a chance to race. In 1928 he won an important race in Japan. The crowd were amazed to see him keep on running out of the sports ground and into a taxi. He had only fifteen minutes to catch his boat back to China. The ship had left the jetty when he arrived. Eric made a huge leap and landed on the deck!

In his own country Eric Liddell was not forgotten. In 1942 people all over Scotland were very sad to hear that the "Flying Scot" had died in China.

Index